FlyHigh 3
Fun Grammar

Contents

Hello, girls and boys!

Hello, girls and boys! How are you?

This is Rob and this is Vicky. They're our friends. Welcome to our zoo!

1 Answer. Then draw and answer about you.

 1 What's her name?
Her name is Sally.

 2 What's his name?
....

 3 What's her name?
....

 4 What's your name?
....

2 Choose and write.

fine   ~~Hello~~   How   Vicky   I'm (x2)   you   thank   are

Rob: (1) Hello ! (2) .... Rob.
Sally: Hello, Rob! How (3) .... you?
Rob: I'm (4) ...., thank you. This is my sister, (5) ....
Sally: (6) .... are (7) ...., Vicky?
Vicky: (8) .... fine, (9) .... you.

3 Find and write.

1-a	2-b	3-c	4-d	5-e	6-f	7-g	8-h	9-i	10-j	11-k	12-l	13-m
14-n	15-o	16-p	17-q	18-r	19-s	20-t	21-u	22-v	23-w	24-x	25-y	26-z

20 8 5   1 14 9 13 1 12 19   1 18 5   25 15 21 18   6 18 9 5 14 4 19

_ _ _   _ _ _ _ _ _ _   _ _ _   _ _ _ _   _ _ _ _ _ _ _.

23 5 12 3 15 13 5   20 15   20 8 5   26 15 15

_ _ _ _ _ _ _   _ _   _ _ _   _ _ _!

Let's Sing  Track 3

Listen and write.

English   friends   ~~animals~~   books   zoo   girls

Hello, girls and boys,
Hello to you.
We are the (**1**) ......animals...... in the zoo.
We're your friends and
we are here.
We're learning (**2**) .... all the year.

Hello, (**3**) .... and boys,
Hello to you.
We're your (**4**) .... here in the zoo.
We like songs and
(**5**) .... and fun.
Let's learn English, everyone!

Hello, girls and boys,
Hello to you.
Welcome to our (**6**) ....!

1 be: affirmative and negative

I'm Karla. I'm a kangaroo.

They're from Africa.

We're on holiday!

Track 4

Affirmative		Negative	
Long forms	**Short forms**	**Long forms**	**Short forms**
I am	I'm	I am not	I'm not
You/We/They are	You/We/They're	You/We/They are not	You/We/They aren't
He/She/It is	He/She/It's	He/She/It is not	He/She/It isn't

1 Write.

Long forms

1 I am from England.
2 You are my friend.
3 She is at the zoo.
4 I am not shy.
5 You are not my cousin.
6 He is not on holiday.

Short forms

I'm from England.
.... my friend.
.... at the zoo.
.... shy.
.... my cousin.
.... on holiday.

2 Read and write.

1 Rob is a boy.
2 Vicky is a girl.
3 Ziggy and his family are from Africa.
4 My cousin and I are nine.
5 You and Mary are friends.
6 The flowers are red.

He's a boy.
.... a girl.
.... from Africa.
.... nine.
.... friends.
.... red.

3 Correct the sentences.

1 Ziggy is from England. He _isn't_ from England. _He's_ from Africa.
2 Trumpet and Ziggy are cousins. They .... cousins. .... friends.
3 Vicky is a boy. She .... a boy. .... a girl.
4 Rosa and I are at the zoo. We .... at the zoo. .... at school.
5 London is in Africa. It .... in Africa. .... in England.
6 Karla and Chatter are children. They .... children. .... animals.

Are you shy?

No, I'm not.

Track 5

Questions	Short answers
Am I …?	Yes, you are./No, you aren't.
Are you …?	Yes, I am./No, I'm not.
Is he/she/it …?	Yes, he/she/it is.
	No, he/she/it isn't.
Are we/you/they …?	Yes, we/you/they are.
	No, we/you/they aren't.

We use short forms to answer No:
    No, I'm not.   No, you aren't.
But we use long forms to answer Yes:
    Yes, I am. ✓   ~~Yes, I'm.~~ ✗

4 Write ? or .

1 Is Ziggy from Africa _?_   2 She isn't shy ......
3 Are you a teacher ......   4 The children are on holiday ......
5 Is Trumpet your cousin ......   6 I'm not his cousin ......

5 Match.

1 Is Tag on holiday?   **a** Yes, he is.
2 Are Ziggy and his family at the airport?   **b** No, it isn't.
3 Is Trumpet hungry?   **c** No, we aren't.
4 Are you happy?   **d** No, he isn't.
5 Is the flag blue?   **e** Yes, they are.
6 Are you and your friends tired?   **f** Yes, I am.

Yes/No questions

6 **Write Is or Are. Then answer.**

1  ....Are.... you hungry?
Yes, I am.

2 .... Tim shy?

3 .... Bob tired?

4  .... they at the zoo?

7 **Write in the correct order. Then answer about you.**

1 hungry? / you / Are
.............Are you hungry?.............

2 from / Australia? / you / and / your / family / Are
....

3 your / dad / Is / a spy?
....

4 Is / the airport? / at / your / mum
....

5 school? / you / Are / at
....

6 happy? / your / friends / Are
....

Let's Sing 🔘 Track 6

Listen and put a ✓. Then answer.

    ✓

Where are you from? ....

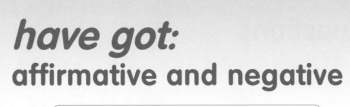

2 *have got:* affirmative and negative

I've got a watch.
I haven't got a mobile phone.

Track 7

Affirmative		Negative	
Long forms	**Short forms**	**Long forms**	**Short forms**
I/You/We/They have got	I/You/We/They've got	I/You/We/They have not got	I/You/We/They haven't got
He/She/It has got	He/She/It's got	He/She/It has not got	He/She/It hasn't got

1 **Look and circle** yes **or** no.

1 Ziggy has got sunglasses.   yes / no
2 His cousin has got a pink swimsuit.   yes / no
3 Tag has got a map.   yes / no
4 Chatter has got black and white clothes.   yes / no
5 Tag has got a camera.   yes / no
6 Karla has got a bag.   yes / no

2 **Listen and put a** ✓ **or** ✗.  Track 8

1 Tim has got a car.   ✓   **2** It's got two doors.   ....
3 It's got a radio.   ....   **4** Betty hasn't got a cat.   ....
5 It's got short legs.   ....   **6** It hasn't got small ears.   ....
7 Daniel has got a robot. ....   **8** It's got two arms and four legs. ....

2 Yes/No questions

Have you got sunglasses?

Yes, I have.
But I haven't got a camera.

Track 9

Questions	Short answers
Have I/you/we/they got …?	Yes, I/you/we/they have.
	No, I/you/we/they haven't.
Has he/she/it got …?	Yes, he/she/it has.
	No, he/she/it hasn't.

3 Write ? or .

1 Has Ziggy got a map ?
2 He hasn't got a radio ......
3 Have you got new clothes ......
4 The girls have got sunglasses ......
5 I haven't got shorts ......
6 Has Sally got a swimsuit ......

4 Look and match.

1 Has Tag got a suitcase?   a No, they haven't.
2 Has Karla got a camera?   b Yes, she has.
3 Has Sally got a ticket?   c Yes, he has.
4 Have Patty and Ziggy got passports?   d No, she hasn't.

5 **Look and write.**

1 Anna and Jack / passports

A: Have Anna and Jack got passports?

B: No, they haven't. They've got sunglasses.

2 Sarah and Mary / a ticket

A: ....

B: ....

3 Sam / a radio

A: ....

B: ....

4 Nelly / a book

A: ....

B: ....

6 **Write in the correct order. Then answer about you.**

1 a / brother? / Have / got / you

Have you got a brother?

....

2 your / dad / a / camera? / Has / got

....

....

3 Have / bikes? / your / got / friends

....

....

4 a / taxi? / got / Has / uncle / your

....

....

5 you / got / Have / passport? / a

....

....

6 mobile phones? / Have / got / your / cousins

....

....

Let's Play (Track 10)

He's got two big ears and a long trunk. Who is he?

He's Trumpet.

Fun Grammar Review 1

1 **Read. Then choose and complete.**

Zebras

Zebras (**1**) ......*are*...... black and white.
Ziggy (**2**) .... a zebra.
He (**3**) .... brown.
Zebras (**4**) .... four legs, two ears and two eyes. They (**5**) .... a long tail.
Ziggy (**6**) .... a long tail too.
Zebras (**7**) .... beautiful animals.
They (**8**) .... small. They live in Africa or in the zoo.

1	have	~~are~~	aren't
2	has	is	isn't
3	haven't	aren't	isn't
4	have got	has got	are
5	isn't	has got	have got
6	have got	is	has got
7	is	have got	are
8	aren't	hasn't got	isn't

2 **Match.**

1 Have you got a cousin?
2 Is she your aunt?
3 Are you at the airport?
4 Has he got Maths on Friday?
5 Are they teachers?
6 Has it got big ears?

a No, she isn't.
b No, it hasn't.
c Yes, they are.
d Yes, I have.
e No, he hasn't.
f Yes, I am.

3 **Choose and write.**

hasn't   isn't   ~~'ve~~   's   got

(**1**) I ....*'ve*.... got a pet. It's a dog. (**2**) It .... big and white. (**3**) It's .... blue eyes.
(**4**) It .... got big ears. It's got small ears. My friend has got a dog too. (**5**) It ....
big. It's small and brown. I love dogs.

4 Look and circle.

  Wednesday

Monday Tuesday Wednesday Thursday

1 They ve got / 's got Maths on Monday.
2 Sarah has got / hasn't got PE on Tuesday.
3 Has / Have you got History on Wednesday?
4 Bob and Tom hasn't got / haven't got English on Thursday.
5 Nick has got / hasn't got Art on Monday.

5 Write in the correct order.

1 you / clever? / Are   Are you clever?
2 blue. / aren't / Monkeys   ....
3 your / funny? / cousin / Is   ....
4 isn't / friend / short. / My   ....
5 and / white. / bag / red / The / is ....

My English

Write and draw. Then colour.

 This is my friend, Kostas.
He's ten. He's tall.
He isn't short. He's got
brown hair and brown
eyes. He's got a parrot.
He hasn't got a cat.

This is ....
....
....
....
....

Now draw a face.

3 Present simple: affirmative

He washes his bike on Saturday.

He watches TV every day.

Track 11

We use the present simple to talk about things we do regularly. To make the present simple with I, you, we and they, we use the main verb. To make it with he, she and it, we usually add -s to the main verb.

I/You/We/They   get up
He/She/It   gets up   at seven o'clock every day.

Remember some verbs are different. We add -es to verbs that end in -o, -sh or -ch.
do → does   go → goes   wash → washes   watch → watches

The verb have is irregular.
I/You/We/They have   He/She/It has

Here are some common time expressions we use with the present simple.
every   day/afternoon/morning/evening/weekend/year
at   six o'clock/night
in   the morning/the afternoon/the evening/winter/spring/summer/autumn

1 **Choose and write. Then listen and repeat.** **Track 12**

~~run~~   ~~watch~~   play   wash   do   look   ride   sing   go   eat

+s	+es
runs	watches

2 **Circle.**

1 I (play) / plays football in the afternoon.

2 He go / goes to school in the morning.

3 She have / has lunch at two o'clock.

4 They watch / watches TV in the evening.

5 You do / does your homework in the afternoon.

6 It open / opens at six o'clock.

3 **Find and write.**

1

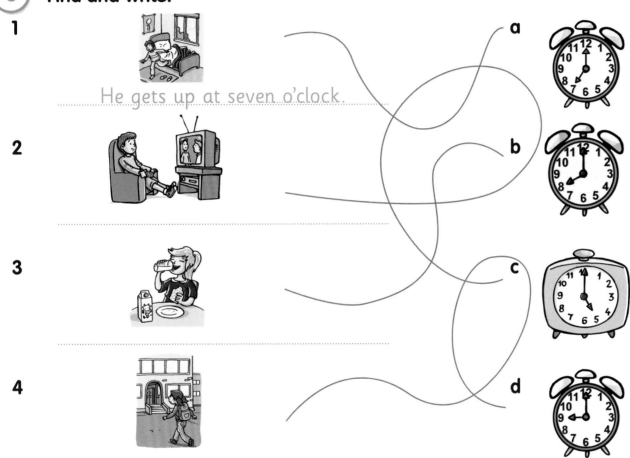

He gets up at seven o'clock.

2

....

3

....

4

....

4 **Choose and write.**

have   read   ~~go~~   play   watch   drink   swim   do   come

Every morning I (**1**) ......go...... to school at eight o'clock. My mum (**2**) .... in the pool and then she (**3**) .... a book. My dad (**4**) .... home for lunch at one o'clock. We all (**5**) .... lunch at two o'clock. Every afternoon my sister (**6**) .... her homework. I (**7**) .... TV and then I play football with my best friend, Sam. He (**8**) .... very well. At eight o'clock I go home. We all (**9**) .... milk and eat pizza in the evening. We go to bed at ten o'clock.

3 Negative and *Yes/No* questions

He doesn't play basketball every day.

Track 13

Long forms

I/You/We/They do not swim every day.
He/She/It does not swim every day.

Short forms

I/You/We/They don't swim every day.
He/She/It doesn't swim every day.

5 Circle.

1 I don't / doesn't get up at six o'clock.

2 He don't / doesn't swim in the evening.

3 We don't / doesn't go to school in summer.

4 The shops don't / doesn't open at six o'clock in the morning.

5 My brother don't / doesn't play in the park every weekend.

6 Lucy don't / doesn't watch TV in the afternoon.

6 Choose and write.

play   ~~get up~~   ride   eat   write   go

1 I _____get up_____ at seven o'clock. I ____don't get up____ at eight o'clock.

2 We _____ to school every day. We _____ to the zoo.

3 My brother _____ football. He _____ volleyball.

4 My dad _____ pizza in the evening. He _____ it for breakfast.

5 We _____ our bikes in the park. We _____ our bikes in the house.

6 I _____ postcards on holiday. I _____ postcards at home.

Does she come from China?

Yes, she does.

 Track 14

We also use the present simple to talk about facts.

Questions	Short answers
Do I/you/we/they eat fish?	Yes, I/you/we/they do.
	No, I/you/we/they don't.
Does he/she/it eat fish?	Yes, he/she/it does.
	No, he/she/it doesn't.

When we make questions with Does, we don't add -s or -es to the main verb.

Does she come from England? ✓   ~~Does she comes from England?~~ ✗

7   **Write** Do **or** Does. **Then answer.**

1

...Does... John wake up at six o'clock?
No, he doesn't.

2

.... Daisy like orange juice?
....

3

.... pandas eat meat?
....

4

.... they live in a house?
....

3 Negative and *Yes/No* questions

8 **Write** do, does, don't **or** doesn't.

Sally: (**1**) ....Do........ you like Maths?

Rob: Yes, I (**2**) ......do...... .

Sally: (**3**) .... your friend, Bob, like Maths too?

Rob: Yes, he (**4**) .... And he likes History. But he (**5**) .... like Art.

Sally: (**6**) .... you and Rob go to the park every Saturday?

Vicky: Yes, we (**7**) .... Rob and I ride our bikes.

Rob: (**8**) .... you ride a bike, Sally?

Sally: No, I (**9**) .... But I swim every Saturday. (**10**) .... your teacher swim every Saturday?

Rob and Vicky: No, she (**11**) ....

9 **Answer about you.**

1 Do you like Maths? ....

2 Do you like History? ....

3 Do you like Art? ....

4 Do you swim every Saturday? ....

Let's Sing 🔘 Track 15

Listen and put a ✓. Then write.

On holiday Ziggy …

1 plays on the beach   ✓   Ziggy plays on the beach.

2 wakes up at six o'clock   ......   He doesn't wake up at six o'clock.

3 watches TV   ....

4 swims in the sea   ....

5 does homework   ....

6 takes photos   ....

4 Present simple:
Adverbs of frequency

I sometimes take photos.

Track 16

We use adverbs of frequency to talk about how regularly we do things.

always ●   sometimes ◑   never ○

We use adverbs of frequency before the main verb in the sentence.

I always go to school.

I sometimes go to the park.

I never go to the zoo.

1   **Listen and look. Then circle.**   Track 17

1 always / sometimes

2 in the afternoon / in the evening

3 sometimes / always

4 at night / in the evening

2   **Write** always, sometimes **or** never.

1 He ___always___ (●) goes to bed at ten o'clock.

2 She _____ (◑) reads a book.

3 We _____ (○) play football in the house.

4 They _____ (◑) walk to school.

5 The fish _____ (○) eats ice cream.

6 I _____ (●) get up early.

4 Adverbs of frequency

3 Circle.

1 He cleans his teeth (in the morning) / always.
2 Mary always / every day does her homework.
3 They in the afternoon / sometimes sleep late.
4 We have breakfast sometimes / in the morning.
5 Grandma always / every morning gets up early.
6 I go to school never / every day.

4 Write.

1 Kim doesn't go to school. (at the weekend)
   Kim doesn't go to school at the weekend.
2 She eats cherries. (never)
   ....
3 They play football. (every day)
   ....
4 They get up at eight o'clock. (always)
   ....
5 Jane swims in the river. (sometimes)
   ....
6 Do you drink milk? (in the afternoon)
   ....

5 Write.

1 he / sometimes / read / books (✓)   He sometimes reads books.
2 they / get up / early / in the morning (?) ....
3 we / swim / in the river (✗)   ....
4 the dog / play / with the ball (✗)   ....
5 I / always / drink milk (✓)   ....
6 she / eat / apples (?)   ....

6 Write in the correct order.

1 Mum / in the evening. / dishes / washes / the

Mum washes the dishes in the evening.

2 bike. / Peter / sometimes / his / rides

....

3 every / Friday. / don't / tennis / Bob and Sam / play

....

4 always / chase / Dogs / cats.

....

5 you / every day? / grandpa / your / visit / Do

....

6 a shower / We / in the morning. / have

....

7 Put a ✓ and write about you.

	always	sometimes	never
wake up late			
drink milk			
read books			
go to the supermarket			

1 ....

2 ....

3 ....

4 ....

Let's Chat Track 18

I sometimes eat bananas.

I always eat bananas.

Fun Grammar Review ②

1 Read and answer.

This is Carol. She's eight. She lives in a big house with her family. Carol goes to school every day at eight o'clock in the morning. At one o'clock she does her homework. In the afternoon she sometimes goes to the park with her friends. They usually ride their bikes and they play volleyball.

Every morning the postman comes to her house at seven o'clock. He usually has some letters for Carol but today he's got a parcel. It's a photo album from her cousin, Mary. She's on holiday in Turkey.

1 Does Carol live in a big house? .... Yes, she does. ....
2 Does she go to school at nine o'clock? ....
3 Do Carol and her friends ride their bikes in the park? ....
4 Do they usually play tennis? ....
5 Does the postman come at eight o'clock every morning? ....
6 Does he usually have letters for Carol? ....

2 Write.

1 I .... have .... (have) breakfast every day.
2 Tina .... (watch) TV in the evening.
3 My friend .... (ride) his bike in the park.
4 Lions .... (run) very fast.
5 They .... (come) from Russia .

3 Circle and write.

1 (Do) / Does you go to school in September? _____ Yes, I do.
2 Do / Does pandas eat leaves? _____
3 Do / Does Ziggy come from Africa? _____
4 Do / Does it snow in August? _____
5 Do / Does fish live in the forest? _____

4 Write don't or doesn't.

1 It _____ doesn't _____ snow in summer.
2 Pandas _____ come from England.
3 A tiger _____ have leaves for breakfast.
4 Bob and Mary _____ like meat.
5 The postman _____ come on Sundays.

5 Choose always, sometimes or never. Then write about you.

1 go / school / in summer _____
2 play / park / in spring _____
3 do homework / in the afternoon _____
4 have spaghetti / for lunch _____

My English

Write about your friend.

My friend, Eleni, goes to school in the morning. She comes home at two o'clock and she has lunch. In the afternoon she does her homework and she sometimes goes for a walk with her mum.

My friend, _____
_____ .
_____
_____
_____

Now draw a face.

5 Present continuous:
affirmative and negative

I'm playing basketball.

We use the present continuous to talk about something that is happening now. We make the present continuous with am, is, are + a verb with -ing.

Long forms	**Short forms**
I am talking.	I'm talking.
You/We/They are talking.	You/We/They're talking.
He/She/It is talking.	He/She/It's talking.

When the verb ends in -e, we drop the -e and add -ing.

dance + ing → dancing   take + ing → taking

When a verb of one syllable ends with a vowel and a consonant, we sometimes double the consonant and add -ing.

swim + ing → swimming   run+ ing → running

1 Circle.

1 Mary is / are swimming.
2 The children is / are watching TV.
3 I is / am walking to school.
4 We are / am having lunch.
5 The dog am / is chasing the cat.
6 Bob is / are eating an apple.

2 Write.

1 She 's playing the guitar. (play)
2 They _____ a new song. (learn)
3 The doorbell _____ . (ring)
4 Rob _____ to his friend. (talk)
5 Vicky _____ a birthday cake. (make)
6 We _____ to the singing. (listen)

She isn't washing the dishes.

Long forms
I am not walking.
You/We/They are not walking.
He/She/It is not walking.

Short forms
I'm not walking.
You/We/They aren't walking.
He/She/It isn't walking.

3 **Look and write.**

1

Mum __is__ cooking.
She __isn't__ dancing.

2

Rob and Sam _____ talking.
They _____ reading

3

Mary _____ riding a bike.
She _____ learning a new song.

4

Bob _____ washing his bike.
He _____ washing the car.

4 **Match and write.**

1 Rob is tasting a strawberry.
2 Betty and I are learning English.
3 The girl is cleaning the floor.
4 Tom and Sam are playing football.
5 I'm cooking breakfast.
6 My aunt is making a dress.

a They _____ volleyball.
b She _____ a hat.
c I _____ lunch.
d He ____isn't tasting____ an apple.
e We _____ History.
f She _____ her room.

Yes/No questions

Is he going to the cinema?

No, he isn't. He's shopping at the supermarket.

Track 21

Questions	**Short answers**
Am I running?	Yes, you are./No, you aren't.
Are you running?	Yes, I am./No, I'm not.
Is he/she/it running?	Yes, he/she/it is./No, he/she/it isn't.
Are we/you/they running?	Yes, we/you/they are./No, we/you/they aren't.

5 Write the questions. Then answer.

1 she / walk
Is she walking? Yes, she is.

2 he / go / to the library
.... No, ...

3 they / buy / books
.... Yes, ...

4 you / make / a cake
.... No, ...

6 Write Is or Are. Then answer.

1    Is she riding a bike?
Yes, she is.

2   .... he buying food?
....

3   .... she cooking?
....

4    .... they running?
....

7 **Write.**

1 wear / blue sweater
   Is he wearing a blue sweater?
       Yes, he is.

2 go / to the library
   ....
   ....

3 carry / a suitcase
   ....
   ....

4 go / to the cinema
   ....
   ....

8 **Write in the correct order. Then answer about you.**

1 painting? / you / Are
       Are you painting?
   ....

2 writing / you / and / postcards? /
   your friends / Are
   ....
   ....

3 your dad / sleeping? / Is
   ....
   ....

4 Is / talking? / your teacher
   ....
   ....

 **Let's Sing** ⊙ Track 22

Listen and write.

~~cook~~   eat   have   clean

(**1**) We 're cooking in the kitchen.
We are having lots of fun.
We are making a cake
To eat with everyone.

(**2**) We .... up the kitchen.
(**3**) We .... lots of fun.
We are eating the cake.
(**4**) We .... every crumb!

Yum, yum! Yum, yum!
We're eating every crumb!

Imperatives:
Let's/Don't

Track 23

We use Let's to suggest to someone that you do something together.

  Let's go to the cinema.

We use the imperative to tell someone to do something or not to do something. To make affirmative imperatives, we use the main verb at the start of a sentence. For negatives, we use Don't before the main verb.

Affirmative	**Negative**
Stand up.	Don't stand up.
Stop.	Don't stop.
Open the window.	Don't open the window.

1 **Listen and number.**   Track 24

a b c d e

| 1 | | | | |

2 Match.

1 I'm hungry.   a Open the window.
2 There's a snake.   b Let's help.
3 We're in the library.   c Let's make a sandwich.
4 I'm bored.   d Run!
5 My mum is making a cake.   e Don't talk.
6 It's hot.   f Let's go to the cinema.

3 Write Let's or Don't.

1 It's my birthday. _____Let's_____ make a cake.
2 The bus is coming. _____ run.
3 _____ play football in the classroom.
4 It's time for lunch. _____ eat pizza.
5 It's eleven o'clock at night. _____ go to the park.
6 It's Saturday. _____ play all day.

4 Choose and write.

eat   play   clean   help   make   wash

1 _____Help_____ your mum.   2 _____Don't eat_____ food in the living room.
3 _____ a mess.   4 _____ the dishes.
5 _____ football in class.   6 _____ your room.

Let's Chat   Track 25

I'm bored.

Let's go to the cinema!

Fun Grammar Review ③

1 Listen and draw lines.  Track 26

Fred   Kim   Lucy

Jane   Anna   Peter

2 Write.

1 The children are waiting (wait) for the bus.
2 The girl _____ (feed) the monkeys.
3 Tom _____ (not play) basketball in the park.
4 The boys _____ (not go) shopping.
5 _____ Vicky _____ (talk) on the phone?
6 _____ the cats _____ (drink) milk?

3 Write in the correct order.

1 are / police / The / chasing / thief. / the
   The police are chasing the thief.

2 cooking / lunch. / is / Mum
   ....

3 running? / he / Is
   ....

4 the / Close / please. / window
   ....

5 man / fighting / isn't / the / bear. / The

6 sit / desk. / on / Don't / the
   ....

4 Choose and write. Use Let's or Don't.

read   play   swim   feed

1

Let's read a book.

2

.... in the river.

3

.... the goats.

4

.... football in the park.

5 Write Is or Are. Then answer about you.

1 Are you writing?   ....

2 .... your teacher waiting for the bus?   ....

3 .... your mum and dad chasing a thief?   ....

4 .... it raining?   ....

5 .... your teacher reading?   ....

6 .... your friends riding their bikes?   ....

My English

Write.

I'm making a cake. I'm not washing the dishes. My friend, Tina, is reading a book. She isn't doing her homework.

I'm .... I'm not .... My friend,

..................., ...

Now draw a face.

7 Possessive adjectives:
my, your, his, her, its, our, your, their

He's Trumpet. This is his car.

 Track 27

| Personal pronouns | Possessive adjectives | We use possessive adjectives to show that someone owns something. We usually use a noun after a possessive adjective.

This is his towel. |
|---|---|---|
| I | my | |
| you | your | |
| he | his | |
| she | her | |
| it | its | |
| we | our | |
| you | your | |
| they | their | |

1 **Write and colour.**

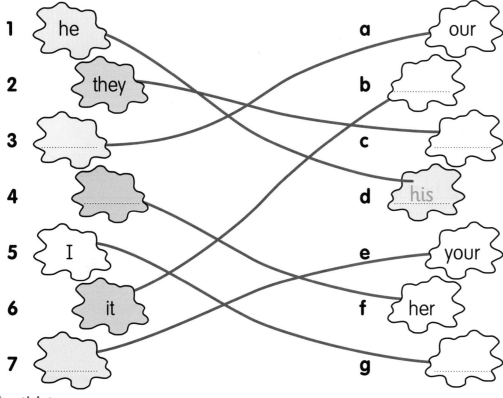

1 he   a our

2 they   b ....

3 ....   c ....

4 ....   d his

5 I   e your

6 it   f her

7 ....   g ....

2 Choose and write.

my   Your   ~~My~~   his   her   its   our   their

1 I'm a teacher. __My__ school is new.

2 I'm a boy and this is _____ bike.

3 This is Mary and that is _____ book.

4 You're a girl. _____ bag is pink.

5 We're friends. This is _____ treehouse.

6 They're monkeys and this is _____ food.

7 This is a cat and that is _____ ball.

8 He's Nick and this is _____ mum.

3 Look and write.

1  I'm Anna. _My sunglasses_ are new.

2  He's Peter. .... is green.

3  They've got a dog. .... is small.

4  She's Lucy. .... is red.

4 Write His or Her.

1 __His__ sunglasses are black.
2 _____ bike is red.
3 _____ T-shirt is pink.
4 _____ trousers are blue.
5 _____ ball is black and white.
6 _____ guitar is brown.

Let's Chat 🔘 Track 28

I'm Chatter and these are my sunglasses. He's Tag and this is his camera.

7 Whose ...?, 's

Whose is this leg?

It's Chatter's leg.

Track 29

To show that someone owns something, we use - 's.
This is John's bike.
We use Whose ...? to ask who owns something. To answer we use a name + 's or a possessive adjective.

Singular	**Plural**
Whose is this pen?	Whose are these shoes?
It's Mary's pen.	They're Ben's shoes.
It's her pen.	They're his shoes.

5 Circle.

1 This is Anna's / Anna radio.
2 My mum / mum's skirt is red.
3 Whose are these sunglasses?
They're Kim's / Kim.
4 Whose / Who is this shirt?
6 Ben's / Ben computer game is new.
5 This is my friend / friend's suitcase.

6 Write in the correct order. Then match.

1 pen? / this / Whose / is
   Whose is this pen?

2 trumpet? / this / is / Whose
   ....

3 are / shoes? / Whose / these
   ....

4 dog? / Whose / this / is
   ....

5 sweets? / these / are / Whose
   ....

6 is / Whose / this / swimsuit?
   ....

a They're Sam's sweets.

b It's Betty's dog.

c It's Mum's swimsuit.

d They're Ellie's shoes.

e It's Tom's pen.

f It's Dad's trumpet.

7 **Find and write.**

1 Whose is this ticket?
   It's Jack's ticket.

2 Whose are these shorts?
   ....

3 Whose is this towel?
   ....

4 Whose is this map?
   ....

5 Whose are these sunglasses?
   ....

6 Whose is this swimsuit?
   ....

8 **Write the questions. Then answer.**

1 Mike   Whose is this trumpet?
             It's Mike's trumpet.

2 Amy   ....
             ....

3 Steve   ....
             ....

4 Sandra ....
             ....

Let's Play   Track 30

Whose is this tambourine?

It's Patty's.

8 Countable and uncountable nouns: *some/any*

> There are some bananas but there aren't any cherries.

We use some in affirmative sentences.

> There are some sweets.

We use any in negative sentences and questions.

> There aren't any sweets.
> Are there any sweets?
> Yes, there are some sweets./No, there aren't any sweets.

1 Circle.

1 There isn't some / (any) milk.
2 Are there some / any straws?
3 There is some / any flour.
4 There aren't some / any towels.
5 There are some / any watermelons.
6 Is there some / any orange juice?

2 Write.

1 we / / (✓)   We've got some peaches.

2 we / / (✗)   We haven't got any cherries.

3 we /  / (?)   ....

4 we / / (✓)   ....

5 we /  / (?)   ....

6 we / / (✗)   ....

There are two peaches.
There is some sugar.

Countable nouns	Uncountable nouns
• Nouns we can count.	• Nouns we can't count.
• We use them in the singular and plural.	• We use them only in the singular.
• We can use a, an or a number before a countable noun.	• We can't use a, an or a number before an uncountable noun.

3 **Choose and write.**

~~water~~   ~~apple~~   butter   biscuit   peach   milk   honey   sweet   flour

egg   spaghetti   banana   orange   cherry   sugar   cheese   watermelon

Countable

apple

Uncountable

water

4 **Write a, an or some.**

1 There is ___an___ orange on the table.
2 There is _____ water in the glass.
3 There is _____ peach in the bowl.
4 There is _____ flour in the bag.
5 There is _____ egg in the fridge.
6 There is _____ butter on the dish.

8 *much/many/lots of*

How much honey is there?

There is lots of honey!

Track 33

We use many and How many...? with countable nouns. We usually use many in negative sentences. We use How many…? to ask questions.

How many books are there? There aren't many books.

We use much and How much...? with uncountable nouns. We usually use much in negative sentences. We use How much…? to ask questions.

How much milk is there? There isn't much milk.

We use lots of with countable and uncountable nouns, usually in affirmative sentences.

There are lots of peaches.   There is lots of sugar.

5 Listen and put a ✓ or a ✗.   **Track 34**

1 There are many eggs. ....✓....
2 There is some flour. ....
3 There isn't much milk. ....
4 There is lots of butter. ....
5 There is lots of sugar. ....
6 There aren't many cherries. ....

6 Write much, many or lots.

1 There aren't ....many.... people in the supermarket.
2 How .... milk is there?
3 There aren't .... eggs in the fridge.
4 How .... biscuits have we got?
5 There is .... of sugar.
6 There isn't .... butter.

7 **Choose and write.**

a   any   some (×3)
much   ~~many~~   lots   an

Fred: How (**1**) ...many... tomatoes
have we got?

Sue: We've got lots of tomatoes.
Is there (**2**) .... spaghetti?

Fred: No, there isn't but we've got (**3**) .... eggs.

Sue: Great. We've got (**4**) .... cheese too.

Fred: How (**5**) .... milk have we got?

Sue: We've got (**6**) .... of milk. We've got (**7**) .... sandwiches too.

Fred: Is there (**8**) .... orange?

Sue: No, there isn't but there is (**9**) .... watermelon.

8 **Write** How much **or** How many. **Then answer about you.**

1 ...How many... stickers have you got?   ....

2 .... pencils are in your bag?   ....

3 .... milk is there in your fridge?   ....

4 .... orange juice do you drink?   ....

5 .... sweets do you eat?   ....

Let's Sing   Track 35

Listen and write yes **or** no.
Have they got any …?

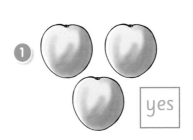 yes

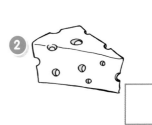

9 Irregular plurals

 Are they mice?

 No, they aren't. They're wolves!

 Track 36

To make the plural of most nouns, we add -s at the end of the word.

car → cars

To make the plural of most nouns that end with -x, -s, -ss, -ch, -sh and -o, we add -es:

fox → foxes   glass → glasses   tomato → tomatoes

bus → buses   dish → dishes

To make the plural of most nouns that end with a -y, we drop the -y and add -ies.

baby → babies   spy → spies

To make the plural of most nouns that end with -f, we drop the -f and add -ves.

wolf → wolves   leaf → leaves

Irregular nouns change in different ways in the plural. Some don't change.

child → children   man → men   sheep → sheep

fish → fish   mouse → mice   tooth → teeth

foot → feet   person → people   woman → women

1 **Listen and number in order. Then write.**  Track 37

 a .... ☐

b .... ☐

c .... ☐

 d .... ☐

e  ....babies.... 1

f .... ☐

2 **Choose and write.**

~~orange~~   wolf   baby   potato   woman   dish   sandwich   person
sweet   shelf   box   foot   leaf   egg   spy   mouse   bus   trumpet

-s	-es	-ies	-ves	irregular
oranges				

3 **Write.**

1 There are ten ……… peaches ……… . (peach)
2 The ……………………… are red. (tomato)
3 The ……………………… are hungry. (wolf)
4 There are two ……………………… in the bathroom. (towel)
5 There are many ……………………… at the park. (person)
6 We've got lots of ……………………… . (strawberry)

4 **Complete the crossword.**

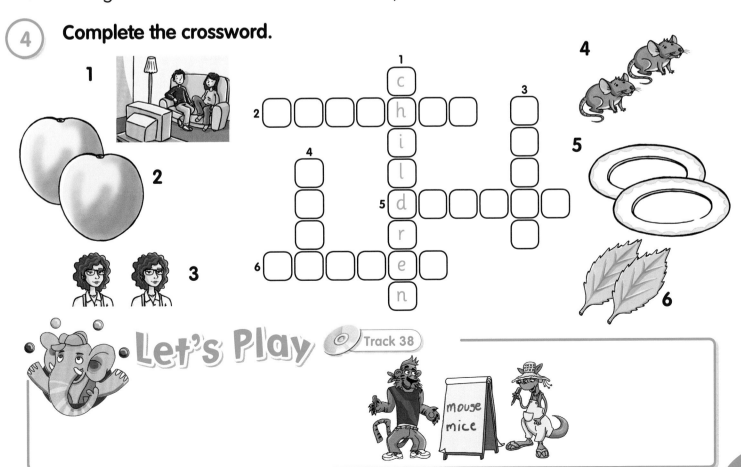

1

2

3

4

5

6

1
c
h
i
l
5 d
r
e
n

2

4

6

3

5

Let's Play   Track 38

mouse
mice

1 Read and write.

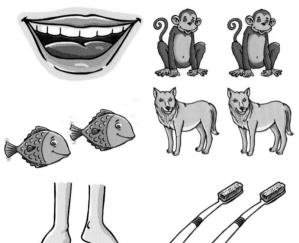

1 We clean our teeth with these. ‎toothbrushes
2 These are in my mouth. ....
3 We all have two of these. ....
4 These animals are very small.
  They like cheese. ....
5 These animals swim in the sea. ....
6 These animals chase sheep. ....

2 Match.

1 I'm John.
2 He's my friend, Peter.
3 My mum is beautiful.
4 This dog is funny.
5 You've got lots of clothes.
6 We are at school.

a Her hair is brown.
b Your shorts are new.
c Our school is old.
d My bike is red.
e Its ears are big.
f His T-shirt is green.

3 Write.

1 Whose is this head?
  It's Patty's head.

2 Whose are these teeth?
  ....

3 ....
  It's Chatter's leg.

4 ....
  They're Karla's feet.

5 Whose is this trunk?
  ....

6 Whose is this arm?
  ....

4 **Choose and write.**

~~sandwich~~   child   leaf   shelf

1 There are two _____sandwiches_____ on the table.
2 There are lots of _____ at school.
3 There are lots of books on _____ in the library.
4 There are lots of _____ on the tree.

5 **Write** some **or** any.

1 There are __some__ oranges in the bowl.   **2** We have got _____ sugar.
3 Are there _____ potatoes?   **4** There aren't _____ straws.

6 **Write** How much **or** How many. **Then match.**

1 __How much__ milk is in the fridge?   **a** There is some.
2 _____ tomatoes are in the bag?   **b** It's got eight legs.
3 _____ butter is in the fridge?   **c** There isn't much.
4 _____ legs has an octopus got?   **d** There are ten.

My English

Write and draw. Then colour.

I've got some butter and some milk.
I haven't got any sugar. I've got some
oranges and peaches. I haven't got
any bananas.

I've got _____ .
I haven't got _____
_____
_____ .

Now draw a face.

10 Comparatives

Karla is taller than Patty.

Track 39

Adjectives are words that describe people, animals or things.

The car is fast.   It's fast.

We use the comparative form of an adjective to compare two people, animals or things. We make the comparative of most adjectives by adding -er to the end of the adjective. We use than after the comparative.

The blue car is faster than the red car.

When an adjective ends in -y, we usually drop the -y and add -ier.

pretty → prettier than   funny → funnier than

When the adjective is one syllable and ends with a vowel and a consonant, we usually double the consonant and add -er.

big → bigger than   sad → sadder than

Irregular adjectives form the comparative in different ways.

good → better than   bad → worse than

1   **Write.**

1   The blue ball is **big** but the red ball is ....bigger........ .

2   The tiger is **strong** but the lion is ....

3   PE is **good** but English is ....

4   Mary is a **bad** singer but Betty is ....

5   Simon is **tall** but Michael is ....

6   Trains are **fast** but planes are ....

2 Put a ✓ or a ✗.

1 Butterflies are smaller than birds. ✓
2 Monkeys are heavier than hippos. ....
3 Tigers are stronger than cats. ....
4 Schools are bigger than houses. ....
5 Cars are faster than planes. ....
6 My grandpa is older than my dad. ....

3 Look and write.

1 Summer is
...... *hotter than* ......
(hot) winter.

2 Maths is
....
(bad) PE.

3 Art is
....
(good) History.

4 A hippo is
....
(heavy) a penguin.

5 A bike is
....
(slow) a train.

6 A strawberry is
....
(small) a watermelon.

4 Write.

I'm at the zoo. Look at the lions – they're running. I love lions. Lions are
(1) .... *faster than* .... (fast) bears. I can see the elephants and the hippos too.
Elephants are (2) .... (heavy) hippos. Here are the kangaroos.
They're (3) .... (big) the monkeys. I love monkeys. They're
(4) .... (funny) the penguins. Look at the snakes. They're playing
with the frogs. Snakes are (5) .... (long) frogs. The zoo is great!

10 Superlatives

> Trumpet is the tallest.

Track 40

We use the superlative form of an adjective to compare a person, an animal or a thing to two or more others. We make the superlative of most adjectives by adding -est to the end of the adjective. We use the before the superlative.

The blue car is the fastest.

When an adjective ends in -y, we usually drop the -y and add -iest.

pretty → the prettiest   funny → the funniest

When the adjective is one syllable and ends with a vowel and a consonant, we usually double the consonant and add -est.

big → the biggest   sad → the saddest

Irregular adjectives form the superlative in different ways.

good → the best   bad → the worst

5 Write.

Adjective	Comparative	Superlative
1 small	smaller than	the smallest
2 young		
3 hot		

Adjective	Comparative	Superlative
4 fat		
5 good		
6 happy		

6 Circle.

1 Whales are the bigger / biggest animals.
2 Tag is thinner / thinnest than Trumpet.
3 Sam's T-shirt is the dirtier / dirtiest.
4 Tigers are heavier / heaviest than mice.
5 This is the worse / worst ice cream.
6 This is the sadder / saddest song.

7 **Choose and write.**

pretty   ~~funny~~   fast   thin

1 The monkey is ___the funniest___ .

2 The red car is _____ .

3 The girl in the orange dress is _____ .

4 The swan is _____ bird.

8 **Write.**

1 I want ___the biggest___ (big) peach in the bowl.

2 Mary is ___taller than___ (tall) Penny.

3 The toy shop is _____ (new) shop in town.

4 A rhino is _____ (heavy) a goat.

5 A baby is _____ (young) a child.

6 He's _____ (good) pupil in the class.

Let's Sing  Track 41

Listen and write.

giraffe   frog   Trumpet   ~~rhino~~   mouse   hippo

1 Who's the funniest?   The rhino   **2** Who's the youngest? _____

3 Who's the tallest? _____   **4** Who's the smallest? _____

5 Who's the fattest? _____   **6** Who's the strongest? _____

11 Past simple: *was/were* affirmative

I was at the playground on Saturday.

Track 42

We use the past simple to talk about the things that happened in the past.

The past simple of the verb be has two main forms: was and were.

Present	Past
I am	I was
You/We/They are	You/We/They were
He/She/It is	He/She/It was

We also use was and were with There.

There is → There was   There are → There were

1 Listen and match. **Track 43**

1

2

3

4

5

6

a

b

c

d

e

f

2 **Circle.**

1 We was /(were) at the playground in the afternoon.

2 He was / were on holiday in July.

3 My friends was / were bored at the library.

4 My dad and my brother was / were at the circus on Saturday.

5 It was a great game. The children was / were excited.

3 **Write.**

1 Sam and Fred are at home. (Monday/school)

 On Monday they were at school.

2 I am tired. (In the morning/hungry)

 ....

3 Today they're at the zoo. (Yesterday/circus)

 ....

4 Dad is happy. (In the afternoon/sad)

 ....

5 Anna is at the beach. (Friday/cinema)

 ....

6 My brother is at the supermarket. (Wednesday/playground)

 ....

4 **Write** was **or** were.

On Sunday it (**1**) ....was........ hot. Everyone (**2**) .... busy. Tag
(**3**) .... in the playground. Karla and Trumpet (**4**) .... at the circus.
There (**5**) .... a lot of people. Patty (**6**) .... at a party. Rob and Vicky
(**7**) .... there too. They (**8**) .... happy. Chatter (**9**) .... in
the park. He (**10**) .... on his rollerblades. Ziggy and his family
(**11**) .... in Turkey. They (**12**) .... on the beach.

11 Negative and *Yes/No* questions

Were you at the zoo on Saturday?

No, I wasn't.

Track 44

Long forms	Short forms
I was not	I wasn't
You/We/They were not	You/We/They weren't
He/She/It was not	He/She/It wasn't

Questions	Short answers
Was I …?	Yes, you were./No, you weren't.
Were you …?	Yes, I was./No, I wasn't.
Was he/she/it …?	Yes, he/she/it was./No, he/she/it wasn't.
Were we/you/they …?	Yes, we/you/they were./No, we/you/they weren't.

Here are some common time expressions we use with the past simple.

yesterday morning/afternoon/evening
this   morning/afternoon/evening
on   Saturday/Sunday

5 Match.

1 Vicky
2 Tag and Chatter
3 Sally wasn't
4 Was Trumpet
5 The animals weren't
6 Were

a happy. She was sad.
b bored? No, he wasn't.
c was at the playground yesterday.
d you at school this morning?
e were sorry about the accident.
f at the zoo. They were at the park.

6 **Write** Was **or** Were**. Then answer.**

1  _____Were_____ they at the beach yesterday?
Yes, they were.

2 _____ Lisa at the airport on Sunday?

3  _____ they at the cinema yesterday evening?

4  _____ Jim tired yesterday morning?

5 _____ there any oranges?

6 _____ the dog under the treehouse?

7 **Answer about you.**

1 Were you at school yesterday morning? _____
2 Was your mum at home yesterday afternoon? _____
3 Were you and your friends at the park on Saturday? _____
4 Was your dad in Turkey last summer? _____
5 Was it sunny yesterday? _____
6 Were you happy yesterday? _____

Let's Play Track 45

Fun Grammar Review  5

1 **Look and write**
yes **or** no.

1 There were six cats in the town yesterday. ...yes...

2 The two cats in the park were sad. ....

3 There weren't lots of cars in the town. ....

4 There weren't lots of flowers in the town. ....

5 The big orange cat wasn't at the supermarket. ....

6 The grey cat was at the toy shop. ....

2 **Circle.**

1 Tigers are (stronger)/ strongest than frogs.

2 Flowers are small / smaller than trees.

3 Dad is the taller / tallest in the family.

4 Whales are the biggest / big animals in the world.

5 Sam is the happiest / happy boy at school.

6 Maths is bad / worse than Art.

3 **Write** was, were, wasn't **or** weren't.

1 Last summer Tom ....was........ in China. (✓)

2 He .... in England. (✗)

3 The children .... at home last night. (✓)

4 They .... at school. (✗)

50 fifty

4 Write.

1 Mark is young but Tim is _the youngest_ in the family.
2 Lions are strong. Tigers are _stronger than_ lions.
3 Dogs are funny but monkeys are _____ dogs.
4 Elephants are tall but giraffes are _____ animals in the world.
5 Mary is a good friend but Lucy is my _____ friend.
6 My bike is old but your bike is _____ my bike.

5 Look and write.

1 _Was_ Lisa at school on Monday?
   Yes, she was.
2 _____ she at the library on Tuesday?
   _____
3 _____ Lisa and her friends at the park
on Wednesday afternoon?
   _____
4 _____ Dad at the supermarket on
Thursday? _____
5 _____ Lisa and Angela at the beach on
Friday evening? _____
6 _____ Dad at the zoo on Saturday? _____
7 _____ Lisa at home on Sunday? _____

Lisa's diary	
Monday	school
Tuesday	home
Wednesday	park with friends in the afternoon
Thursday	toy shop with Mum and Dad
Friday	cinema with Angela in the evening
Saturday	zoo with Mum and Dad
Sunday	homework at home

My English

Write.

It was a sunny day yesterday. I was at the park with my friends. We were very happy.

It _____ . I _____

_____ .

Now draw a face.

12 Past simple: regular verbs
affirmative and negative

We cleaned the zoo yesterday.

Track 46

We use the past simple to talk about things we did in the past.
To make the past simple, we add -ed to most verbs.
   I/You/He/She/It/We/They cleaned.

We add -d to verbs that end in -e.
   like → liked   dance → danced

1 **Write.**

1 Mary ___watched___ (watch) TV this morning.

2 The children _____ (wash) the car yesterday.

3 Fred _____ (visit) his cousin yesterday evening.

4 The dog _____ (play) with the ball this morning.

5 My mum and my sister _____ (paint) the wall yesterday.

6 Sam and I _____ (listen) to the radio this afternoon.

2 **Choose and write.**

play   talk   like   chase   ~~climb~~   help

At the weekend I was at the park with my friends. Sam and Bob (**1**) ___climbed___
a tree. Vicky (**2**) _____ on her mobile phone. Tom (**3**) _____ his brother
on his bike. Some girls (**4**) _____ volleyball. The cat (**5**) _____ the mice.
Everyone (**6**) _____ the park.

He didn't play tennis yesterday.

Long forms

I/You/He/She/It /We/They did not walk.

Short forms

I/You/He/She/It /We/They didn't walk.

When we make negative sentences in the past simple with didn't, we don't add -ed or -d to the main verb.

She didn't play in the park. ✓   ~~She didn't played in the park.~~ ✗

3 **Write.**

watch   play   ~~chase~~   cook

1

The cat _didn't chase_ a dog yesterday.

2

They .... volleyball yesterday.

3

Clare .... fish yesterday.

4

Fiona .... TV yesterday evening.

4 **Write.**

At the weekend …

1 Mum .....cleaned..... (clean) the house but she ...didn't cook... (not cook) lunch.

2 Tom .... (wash) his bike but he .... (not watch) TV.

3 Vicky and Rob .... (dance) at the party but they .... (not play) with their friends.

4 The dog .... (chase) the cat but it .... (not climb) a tree.

5 I .... (help) my grandma but I .... (not listen) to the radio.

6 Sally .... (paint) the walls but she .... (not visit) the animals.

12 Yes/No questions

Questions

Did I/you/he/she/it/we/they play?

Short answers

Yes, I/you/he/she/it/we/they did.

No, I/you/he/she/it/we/they didn't.

When we make questions with Did in the past simple, we don't add -ed or -d to the main verb.

Did she talk to her friend? ✓   Did she talked to her friend? ✗

5 Choose and write.

1 Did Sue visit her grandma this morning?
2 Did you talk on the phone this afternoon?
3 Did Peter and Daisy paint the picture?
4 Did the boy help his mum yesterday?
5 Did the kangaroo jump six metres?
6 Did you and your friends dance at the party yesterday?

a Yes, we did.
b No, he didn't.
c Yes, it did.
d No, they didn't.
e Yes, she did.
f Yes, I did.

6 Choose and write. Then answer.

play   listen   cook   clean   work   talk

1 _Did_ Vicky _play_ football at school?   No, _she didn't_ .
2 _____ they _____ lunch yesterday?   Yes, _____ .
3 _____ you _____ on the phone yesterday?   No, _____ .
4 _____ Jack _____ up his bedroom this afternoon?   Yes, _____ .
5 _____ Julie _____ for a newspaper last summer?   Yes, _____ .
6 _____ your aunt and uncle _____ to the radio
yesterday evening?   No, _____ .

7 **Choose and write.**

The girl   ~~The monkeys~~   The boys   The kangaroo   Mum and the boy

~~climb~~   jump   watch   like   walk

1 The monkeys climbed the tree.
2 .... the elephant.
3 .... eight metres.
4 .... the zebra.
5 ....
in the zoo.

8 **Write about you.**

1 Did you listen to the radio yesterday?
2 Did you play in the park yesterday?
3 Did you climb a tree yesterday?
4 Did you walk to school yesterday?
5 Did you help your mum yesterday?
6 Did you clean up your room yesterday?

Let's Sing  Track 49

Listen and number in order.

Yesterday I was at school, ...
And I played with all my friends. ......
Yesterday I walked to school, __1__
We liked our day at our lovely school! ......
And I talked to all my friends. ......
We climbed, we jumped, we played basketball. ......

Yesterday I walked to school, ...
I was happy with my friends. ......
And I laughed with all my friends. ......
Yesterday I was at school, ...

12 Irregular verbs

He ate lots of bananas yesterday.

Track 50

To make the past simple, we add -ed or -d to most verbs. Irregular verbs make the past simple in different ways.

buy → bought	eat → ate	make → made	take → took
come → came	give → gave	read → read	write → wrote
do → did	go → went	see → saw	
drink → drank	have → had	sit → sat	

Affirmative

I/you/he/she/it/we/they drank.

Negative

I/you/he/she/it/we/they didn't drink.

When we make negative sentences with didn't, we use the main verb.

He didn't drink lots of milk. ✓   ~~He didn't drank lots of milk.~~ ✗

Questions

Did I/you/he/she/it/we/they drink?

Short answers

Yes, I/you/he/she/it/we/they did.
No, I/you/he/she/it/we/they didn't.

When we make questions with Did, we use the main verb.

Did he drink lots of milk? ✓   ~~Did he drank lots of milk?~~ ✗

⑨ **Listen and put a ✓ or ✗.**  Track 51

1 Yesterday John was at school. ....✓....   **2** He had Art. ....

3 He painted a basketball picture. ....   **4** He went home at five o'clock. ....

5 His cousin, Helen, was at home. ....   **6** They went to the park. ....

7 Helen bought a dress. ....

10 **Look, choose and write.**

~~buy~~   read   ~~eat~~   see   come   go

1 Dad ____bought____ a watermelon yesterday.

2 Kim ____didn't eat____ ice cream yesterday.

3 The men _____ to the airport yesterday.

4 The postman _____ yesterday.

5 The children _____ the pandas at the zoo.

6 Karen _____ a book.

11 **Write in the correct order. Then answer.**

1 she / go / Did / to school / yesterday?
____Did she go to school yesterday?____
Yes, _____ .

2 read / Did / a book / last night? / he
_____
No, _____ .

3 yesterday? / Did / your homework / do / you
_____
Yes, _____ .

4 a cake / Did / make / yesterday? / your mum
_____
No, _____ .

5 Tom / buy / Did / last Monday? / sweets
_____
Yes, _____ .

6 ice cream / Did / eat / last summer? / they
_____
No, _____ .

Let's Chat   Track 52

Did you drink all the milk?

Yes, I did!

Fun Grammar Review

1 Listen and draw lines. Track 53

What did Lucy do last week?

Monday   Wednesday   Friday   Sunday

Tuesday   Thursday   Saturday

a  b  c d  e f

2 Circle.

1 Did you went / **go** to Spain in August?

2 I play / played tennis at school yesterday.

3 He didn't washed / wash the dishes this morning.

4 Anna give / gave her bike to her friend.

5 Did Paul write / wrote a letter this afternoon?

6 Sam and Tina didn't helped / help their mum yesterday.

3 Write.

1 I .... went .... to school yesterday but I didn't go to the zoo.

2 Fred .... lots of salad but he didn't eat any pizza.

3 Kim liked the party but she .... the food.

4 The elephants .... a shower but they didn't have breakfast.

5 Mum .... at the airport but she didn't work at the zoo.

6 You cooked chicken but you .... spaghetti.

4 Write.

Hello Sally,

How are you? Rob and I are fine. We (**1**) .... *went* .... (go) to the zoo yesterday. We (**2**) .... (see) lots of animals but we (**3**) .... (not see) the snakes. Rob (**4**) .... (give) apples to the elephants.

I (**5**) .... (eat) lots of ice cream. Rob (**6**) .... (drink) some orange juice but he (**7**) .... (not buy) any sandwiches. We (**8**) .... (go) to the shop. Rob (**9**) .... (buy) a toy animal and I (**10**) .... (get) a book. I (**11**) .... (read) my book this morning. We (**12**) .... (have) a wonderful time.

Love
Vicky

5 Answer.

1 Did Mary come to the party? (✓)   .... Yes, she did. ....
2 Did Ben take a photo of the bear? (✗) ....
3 Did you watch TV this evening? (✗)   ....
4 Did they walk to school? (✓)   ....
5 Did the boy play basketball? (✓)   ....
6 Did I give you my photo album? (✗)   ....

My English

Write.

Yesterday I sat in my room and played a computer game. I didn't watch TV. My brother went to the cinema with his friends. He didn't wash his bike.

Yesterday ....
My ....

Now draw a face.

13 Can

Track 54

We use Can to ask for something or to ask for permission to do something.

Questions
Can I/you/he/she/it/we/they play in the park?

Short answers
Yes, I/you/he/she/it/we/they can.
No, I/you/he/she/it/we/they can't.

When we make questions with Can, we use the main verb.
    Can he ride his bike here? ✓   ~~Can he rides his bike here?~~ ✗

1 Match.

1 They did their homework.
2 It's hot and sunny.
3 He's hungry.
4 She's got a bucket and a spade.
5 Your dog is funny.
6 I'm bored.

a Can we go to the beach?
b Can she make a sandcastle here?
c Can I play with it?
d Can they watch TV?
e Can I go to the park?
f Can he have a sandwich?

2 Answer about you.

1 Can you eat in the classroom?
2 Can you draw on the walls at your school?
3 Can the children ride their bikes at your school?
4 Can the children wear shorts at your school?
5 Can you listen to the radio in your bedroom?
6 Can your friends eat ice cream in winter?

3 Write in the correct order.

1 some / please? / juice, / have / Can / I
Can I have some juice, please?

2 Can / bike / ride / here? / I / my
....

3 the bathroom, / Can / go / please? /
I / to
....
....

4 to the park / Can / now? / I go
....
....

4 Choose and write. Then answer.

wear   ~~make~~   go

1 sandcastle / on the beach
Can I make a sandcastle on the beach?   Yes, _you can_.

2 bed / at twelve o'clock
....   No, ...

3 my armbands / in the swimming pool
....   Yes, ...

  **Track 55**

Listen and write.

please   five   ~~play~~   climb   can   go

Can I (**1**) _play_ with my friends, please?
Can I (**2**) .... and climb those trees?
Can I play with my friends, please?
Yes, you (**3**) ....
Do your homework, write and read.
Do your English homework, (**4**) ....

Then you can (**5**) .... the trees.
Yes, you can.
You can go and play outside.
Please be home by half past (**6**) ....
You can have a lovely time.
Yes, you can.

13 *must/mustn't*

You mustn't play basketball here!

 Track 56

We use must/mustn't to talk about what we have to do or don't have to do.

Affirmative

I/you/he/she/it/we/they must help.

Negative

Long form

I/you/he/she/it/we/they must not fight.

Short form

I/you/he/she/it/we/they mustn't fight.

After must/mustn't we use the main verb.

She must look left and right. ✓   ~~She must looks left and right.~~ ✗

He mustn't eat lots of ice cream.✓   ~~He mustn't eats lots of ice cream.~~ ✗

---

5 Listen and put a ✓.  Track 57

Sam must …

1 clean his teeth. ....✓....

2 feed the dog. ....

3 do his homework. ....

Sam mustn't …

4 make a mess. ....

5 wash the dishes. ....

6 play football in his room. ....

6 Circle.

1 We must / (mustn't) sit in the sun.

2 You must / mustn't help your mum.

3 The baby must / mustn't go to bed early.

4 You must / mustn't ride a bike at school.

5 We must / mustn't read lots of books.

6 I must / mustn't write on the walls.

7 **Write** must **or** mustn't.

1 At school: you ...... mustn't ...... write on the desk.
2 In a library: you .... be quiet.
3 In the house: you .... play football.
4 In the sea: you .... swim far.
5 On the road: you .... look left and right.

8 **Choose and write** must **or** mustn't.

sleep   ~~stay~~   clean   eat   run   drink

1 You ...... must stay ...... near the beach.   **2** We .... across the road.
3 I .... my teeth.   **4** The baby .... milk.
5 You .... at school.   **6** We .... lots of salad.

9 **Choose and write.**

In the classroom

~~be quiet~~   eat   sit on the desk   read and write

talk to your friend   listen to your teacher

1 You must be quiet.   **2** ....
3 ....   **4** ....
5 ....   **6** ....

Let's Play   Track 58

You're on the road!

I must look left and right.

14 Object pronouns:
me, you, him, her, it, us, you, them

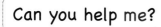

Can you help me?

We use pronouns instead of nouns.

Tim is here. → He's here.

We use object pronouns instead of a noun which is the object of the verb. We usually put them after the main verb.

I can see Tim. → I can see him.

Grandma loves me and my sister. → Grandma loves us.

Subject pronouns	Object pronouns	Subject pronouns	Object pronouns
I	me	it	it
you	you	we	us
he	him	you	you
she	her	they	them

1 Circle.

1 The monkeys are funny. The children like (them) / it.
2 Mum is carrying a heavy bag. Can you help she / her?
3 He's playing basketball. Look at me / him.
4 You and Jack came first in the Olympics. Here's a prize for you / us.
5 I'm skiing! Look at me / I.
6 We're at a party. Come and dance with us / you!

2 Choose and write.

He   us   ~~She~~   her   I   them

1 Sarah likes animals. She has got a cat.   2 I've got a ball. .... can play football.
3 The clowns are funny. Look at ....   4 We can't find the boat. Can you help ....?
5 Sally is kind. I like ....   6 Look at Tom. .... is very sad.

3 Choose and write.

them ~~him~~ you me

1 Look at ___him___ .

2 Can you see _____ ?

3 They're good! Listen to _____ .

4 Happy Birthday! This is for _____ .

4 Match and write.

1 The kangaroos are funny.
2 I can't open the window.
3 Sue and I are going to the park.
4 Where's Peter?
5 Mum is great.
6 I can't draw a plane.

a Can you see _____ ?
b We love _____ .
c Can you help _____ ?
d Do like ___them___ ?
e Can you open _____ ?
f Do you want to come with _____ ?

Let's Chat (Track 60)

I can't do my homework.

I can help you.

15 *will:* affirmative, negative and *Yes/No* questions

We'll be on holiday in August!

August						
			1	2	3	
4	5	6	7	8	9	10
11	12	13	14	15	16	17
18	19	20	21	22	23	24
25	26	27	28	29	30	31

 Track 61

We use will to talk about the future and guess what is going to happen.

Affirmative	**Negative**
Long form	**Long form**
I/you/he/she/it/we/they will swim.	I/you/he/she/it/we/they will not swim.
Short form	**Short form**
I/you/he/she/it/we/they'll swim.	I/you/he/she/it/we/they won't swim.

After will ('ll)/won't we use the main verb.

She'll go to the cinema. ✓   ~~She'll goes to the cinema.~~ ✗

He won't go on holiday. ✓   ~~He won't goes on holiday.~~ ✗

1 Write 'll or won't.

1 I'm hungry. I ___'ll___ make a sandwich. **2** She doesn't like cake. She _____ eat it.
3 I'm tired. I _____ go to bed. **4** It's raining. We _____ go to the beach.
5 He's tired. He _____ come to the party. **6** We like Jo. We _____ play tennis with him.

2 Read and write.

In 50 years people (**1**) __won't clean__ (not clean) their houses. Robots (**2**) __will clean__ (clean) them.

Children (**3**) _____ (not go) to school. They (**4**) _____ (have) lessons at home.

People (**5**) _____ (not swim) in the sea. They (**6**) _____ (go) on holiday to the moon.

Animals (**7**) _____ (not live) in the zoo. They (**8**) _____ (stay) in people's houses.

Will you come to Africa next summer?

Yes, I will.

Questions

Will I/you/he/she/it/we/they go?

Short answers

Yes, I/you/he/she/it/we/they will.

No, I/you/he/she/it/we/they won't.

When we make questions with Will, we use the main verb.

Will he play tennis? ✓   ~~Will he plays tennis?~~ ✗

Here are some common time expressions we use with will.

next   week/weekend/year

in   the morning/the afternoon/the evening

3 **Write.**

Ziggy: Will you come to Africa next summer?

Tag: (1) ....Yes, I will.... (✓) We'll have a wonderful time!

Ziggy: Will your friends come with you?

Tag: (2) .... (✗) They'll visit other places.

Ziggy: Sally likes the mountains. Will she go there?

Tag: (3) .... (✓)

Ziggy: What about Chatter? Will he go to the mountains too?

Tag: (4) .... (✗) He'll go to the beach.

Let's Sing

Listen and write.

1   Will they be sad?   ....No, they won't.......

2   Will they meet again?   ....

3   Will the friends have a lovely holiday? ....

4   Will they do their homework?   ....

5   Will they dive?   ....

Fun Grammar Review ⑦

1 **Listen. Then colour and draw.**  Track 64

2 **Write can or can't.**

Mark: Dad, **(1)** ....can.... I go to the park?

Dad: No, you **(2)** .... It's late. You must do your homework.

Mark: OK, Dad. **(3)** .... I have some pizza?

Dad: Yes, you **(4)** ....

Mark: **(5)** .... I have an ice cream too?

Dad: No, you **(6)** .... But you **(7)** .... have some orange juice.

Mark: Thanks, Dad.

3 **Match.**

1 This T-shirt is dirty.
2 I'm cleaning up my bedroom.
3 We're going to the cinema.
4 Bob is sleeping.
5 You're pretty.
6 I've got lots of cats.

a Don't wake him up.
b I love them.
c Can I take a photo of you?
d Don't wear it.
e Can you help me?
f Are you coming with us?

4 **Choose and write. Use** must **or** mustn't.

sit   eat   g̶o̶   look

1 You ....must go.... to bed.

2 He .... breakfast.

3 You .... left and right.

4 They .... on the desk.

5 **Write. Use** will **or** won't.

1 you / go / shopping / today (**?**) ....Will you go shopping today?.........
2 the girls / play / football (**✗**) ....
3 I / visit / Spain / next summer (**✓**) ....
4 Jack / buy / a new car / next year (**?**) ....
5 it / be / hot and sunny (**✓**) ....
6 she / come / to the party on Saturday (**✗**) ....

My English

Write and draw.

Can I watch TV, Mum?
No, you can't. You must
do your homework.
We'll go to the park in
the afternoon.

Can I .... ?
....
....

Now draw a face.

I can do this! 1

1 **Listen and write.**  Track 65

1 Her name is _____Sarah Walker_____ .
2 She goes to _____ .
3 Today she's got _____ .
4 Her friend, Mary, has got long
   _____ hair.
5 Mary has got _____ eyes.

2 **Look and write** yes **or** no.

1 The girl at the table has got long
   black hair.   ....no....

2 There are two books on the table.
                                        ....

3 The girl in the pink skirt hasn't got
   sunglasses.   ....

4 There's a blue rubber
   on the floor.   ....

5 The boy next to the door
   has got a hat.   ....

6 He hasn't got a map.   ....

3 **Choose and write.**

am   is (×2)   are (×2)   have got (×3)   has got (×2)

1 Fred _____is_____ a boy. He _____has got_____ a blue bike.

2 I _____ at school. I _____ my bag.

3 Helen _____ my cousin. She _____ a doll.

4 We _____ friends. We _____ a treehouse.

5 Sam and Tom _____ brothers. They _____ a big house.

4 **Write in the correct order. Use** always (●)**,** sometimes (◐) **or** never (○)**.**

1 clean / her teeth / in the morning (●)
She _always cleans her teeth in the morning_ .

2 swim / in summer (◐)
They _____ .

3 go / to the cinema / on Monday (○)
He _____ .

4 watch TV / on Sunday (○)
The children _____ .

5 wash / her bike / on Saturday (●)
Kim _____ .

5 **Match.**

1 Have you got a friend?   **a** No, we're not.
2 Is she shy?   **b** No, she hasn't.
3 Are you on holiday?   **c** Yes, I have.
4 Has she got a pet?   **d** Yes, she is.

Hooray!

Draw and colour.

I can do this!

I can do this! 2

1 Read and write.

My name's Ken and this is my family. It's Sunday morning. Dad
(**1**) ....is reading.... (read) his newspaper in the living room. Mum
(**2**) .... (make) breakfast in the kitchen. My sisters, Sarah
and Anna (**3**) .... (chase) the dog in the garden. Grandma
(**4**) .... (watch) TV and I (**5**) .... (write) a letter to
my best friend in Turkey.

2 Circle.

1 He was / were at school today.   2 They wasn't / weren't happy.
3 Were / Was you at the beach?   4 Tania wasn't / weren't bored.
5 Were / Was Rob at the library?   6 Fiona was / were excited yesterday.

3 Choose and write.

some   four   ~~any~~   How many   How much   any

1 There isn't .....any..... butter.   2 There are .... peaches.
3 There is .... sugar.   4 .... milk is there?
5 .... oranges are there?   6 There aren't .... eggs

4 Choose and write.

~~Let's eat!~~   Be quiet!   Let's wash it.   Don't wear your sweater.

1 It's time for lunch .....Let's eat!.....   2 It's hot. ....
3 The car is dirty. ....   4 You're at the library. ....

5 Read and put a ✓ for the correct sentence.

1 **a** The baby are sleeping. ....

    b The baby is sleeping. ✓

2 **a** The boys are playing football every day. ....

    b The boys play football every day. ....

3 **a** Monkeys sometimes are climbing the trees. ....

    b Monkeys sometimes climb trees. ....

4 **a** There isn't any milk in the fridge. ....

    b There isn't some milk in the fridge. ....

5 **a** How much apples have we got? ....

    b How many apples have we got? ....

6 **a** Summer is hotter than winter. ....

    b Summer is hottest than winter. ....

6 Write.

1 Mary / skirt / blue

    Mary's skirt is blue.

2 Tom / shoes / big

3 Nick / shorts / green

4 Sally / trousers / green and orange

7 Write.

1 The red car is ......dirtier than...... (dirty) the blue car.

2 Dinosaurs were ......the biggest...... (big) animals in the world.

3 Sam is .... (tall) John.

4 This is .... (good) cinema in town.

5 Jessica is .... (young) Emily.

6 August is .... (hot) month of the year.

Hooray!

Draw and colour.

I can do this!

I can do this! 3

1 Read and write. Use one or two words.

Yesterday morning Lisa and her brother Ben went to the beach. It was hot and sunny. They sat under the umbrella. Then they played volleyball near the sea. They were very hot. They went for a swim. Their mum was in the sea.

1 Lisa and Ben went to the beach ......yesterday...... .

2 It was .... sunny.

3 They sat under the umbrella and then they .... near the sea.

Then they saw a big thing in the water. It was green. They were scared. Was it a shark? No, it wasn't a shark. It was a big turtle. The turtle was tired. Mum said, 'Let's help it.'

4 Lisa and Ben were ....

5 They saw a .... in the water.

6 The children and their mum .... the turtle.

Some fishermen helped Ben and Lisa to get the turtle out of the water. The turtle was safe. Ben and Lisa looked after the turtle. In the evening they put it in the sea. The turtle looked at them and dived into the water. They had a wonderful time.

7 The .... them to get the turtle out of the water.

8 Ben and Lisa .... the turtle all day.

9 The turtle was safe and .... into the water.

2 Circle.

1 He didn't (eat) / ate the cake.

2 Did she go / went to school?

3 My dad play / played the guitar last night.

4 Did / Do you like the game today?

5 I didn't run / ran in the race last week.

6 I help / helped my mum everyday.

3 Write.

1 She _____listened_____ (listen) to the radio yesterday.
2 Tom and Peter _____ (not play) volleyball in the park yesterday.
3 _____ the dog _____ (eat) the cake yesterday evening?
4 We _____ (do) our homework yesterday.

4 Match and write.

1 The boys are playing.
2 I'm going to the zoo.
3 This is a very big house.
4 It's your birthday.
5 The woman is dancing.
6 We're washing the dishes.

a This is for _____ .
b Can you help _____ ?
c Let's watch _____ .
d Can you see _____them_____ ?
e Do you want to come with _____ ?
f Look at _____ .

5 Write must or mustn't.

1 The boys _____mustn't_____ run in the cinema.
2 Children _____ fight in class.
3 She _____ help her mum clean the car.
4 I _____ eat chocolate for breakfast.
5 We _____ be quiet in class.

6 Write about you.

1 Will you go to school in autumn? ....
2 Will you be fourteen next year? ....
3 Will you go on holiday in August? ....
4 Will you make a cake this evening? ....

Hooray!

Draw and colour.

I can do this!

Look what I can do!

1 **Listen and circle.** Track 66

1 a   b   c

2 a   b   c

3 a   b   c

4 a   b   c

2 **Write.**

Hello I'm Betty. It's Saturday and I'm at the park with my friends. We (**1**) _____'re riding_____ (ride) our bikes.

A woman (**2**) _____ (feed) the birds. Two men (**3**) _____ (read) newspapers.

Three girls (**4**) _____ (talk) and a boy (**5**) _____ (climb) a tree.

3 Read and circle.

1 Billy: Did you go to the beach last Sunday?
Emily: a Yes, I went with my sister.
        b No, it was Friday.
        c Yes, I went to the zoo.

2 Billy: Did you swim?
Emily: a Yes, I want.
        b Yes, they did.
        c Yes, I did. It was great!

3 Billy: Did you play tennis?
Emily: a No, I didn't.
        b I was tired.
        c Yes, we made a sandcastle.

4 Billy: Was it hot and sunny?
Emily: a No, it is worse.
        b Yes, it is.
        c Yes, it was.

5 Billy: Will you go again next Sunday?
Emily: a Yes, I will.
        b Great.
        c No, I don't.

6 Billy: Do you want my bucket and spade?
Emily: a No, I didn't.
        b Yes, please.
        c Yes, I have.

4 Read and write.

1 You can buy food and lots of things in this shop. ....supermarket........
2 You wash your hair with this.
....
3 We put the butter, the milk, the eggs and some food in it.
....
4 You eat from it. ....
5 You can make sandcastles with these.
....
6 You wear it in the sun.
....

Look what I can do!

5 Read and answer. Write sentences.

Hello! I'm Tania. On holiday I get up late so I have breakfast every morning at ten o'clock. My sister gets up late too. We always ride our bikes in the morning. We sometimes go to the park and climb trees.
On Saturday we go to the beach with Mum and Dad. We love swimming. My sister always plays tennis with my mum at the beach. I love holidays!

1 Does Tania get up late on holiday?
Yes, she does.

2 Does she have breakfast at nine o'clock?
No, she has breakfast at ten o' clock.

3 Do Tania and her sister play tennis at the park?
....

4 Do they climb trees?
....

5 Does Tania go to the beach on Saturday?
....

6 Do Tania and her mum ride their bikes at the beach?
....

6 Choose and write.

don't   Do (×2)   Does   doesn't (×2)

1 ....._Do_..... lions eat fruit?

2 They .... do their homework in the evening.

3 She .... eat spaghetti.

4 .... he play the drums?

5 Mark .... drink milk.

6 .... your friends go to the cinema on Saturday?

7 Match.

1 My T-shirt was big.
2 Tina was tall.
3 The baby was happy.
4 The man was thin.
5 They were at the library yesterday.
6 We were busy in the morning.

a It wasn't sad.
b He wasn't fat.
c It wasn't small.
d We weren't bored.
e She wasn't short.
f They weren't at the cinema.

8 **Choose and write.**

close   ~~watch~~   help   go   read   buy

1 My friends and I ___watched___ TV yesterday evening.

2 Mum _____ new shoes.

3 The boy _____ his friend carry the bags.

4 Helen _____ to a party on Saturday.

5 The supermarket _____ early yesterday.

6 I _____ a good book on Sunday.

9 **Write.**

1 Monday is the f i r s t day.

2 Tuesday is the s _ _ _ _ d day.

3 Wednesday is the t _ _ _ d day.

4 Thursday is the f _ _ _ _ h day.

5 Friday is the f _ _ _ h day.

6 Saturday is the s _ _ _ h day.

7 Sunday is the l _ _ t day.

10 **Answer about you.**

1 Do you swim in August? ....

2 Do you and your friends go to school in July? ....

3 Did you go to the beach last summer? ....

4 Did your friends go to the mountains last Sunday? ....

5 Will you ski in January? ....

6 Will you and your family visit Spain in September? ....

7 Will you visit your grandma next weekend? ....

8 Will you go to the library this evening? ....

Hooray!

Draw and colour.

I can do this!

Pearson Education Limited
Edinburgh Gate
Harlow
Essex CM20 2JE
England
and Associated Companies throughout the world.

www.pearsonlongman.com

First published 2011
Thirteenth impression 2022

ISBN: 978-1-4082-4976-5

Printed in Slovakia by Neografia

Set in VagRounded

Illustrated by: GS Animation/Grupa Smacznego,
Christos Skaltsas/eyescream (hyphen),
Juan Noailles (Eclipse Gráfica Creativa)
HL Studios, Long Hanborough, Oxford